D1058760

THE
AMERICAN SADDLEBRED HORSE

by Charlotte Wilcox

C A P S T O N E   P R E S S
M A N K A T O

C A P S T O N E   P R E S S
818 North Willow Street • Mankato, MN 56001

Library of Congress Cataloging-in-Publication Data
Wilcox, Charlotte.
    The American saddlebred horse/by Charlotte Wilcox; reading consultant,
    John Manning.
    p. cm.
    Includes bibliographical references (p. 46) and index.
    Summary: Discusses the lineage, physical characteristics, life span,
    breeding, and uses of the American saddlebred, considered to be one of
    the most beautiful horses in the world.
    ISBN 1-56065-364-7
    1. American saddlebred horse--Juvenile literature. [1. American
saddlebred horse. 2. Horses. 3. Horse breeds.] I. Title.
SF293.A5W54 1996
636.1'3--dc20

                                            95-45142
                                               CIP
                                                AC

Photo credits
American Saddlebred Horse Association: 6, 14, 38
ASHA/Jamie Donaldson: 8, 9, 12, 15, 22-28, 33-36, 41-42
ASHA/Linda Wollaber: 10, 19-20, 30
ASHA/Polly Knoll: 16
Kimberly K. Kiewel: cover

Table of Contents

Words in **boldface** type in the text are defined in the Glossary in the back of this book.

Quick Facts about the American Saddlebred Horse

Description

Height: Saddlebreds are 15 to 16 **hands** from the ground to the top of the shoulders. That is 60 to 64 inches (152 to 163 centimeters) tall. Horses are measured in hands. One hand equals four inches (10 centimeters).

Weight: Saddlebreds weigh 1,000 to 1,200 pounds (450 to 540 kilograms).

Physical features: The Saddlebred has a long, arched neck with head carried high; straight face line; long legs with a high stepping action; and a level **croup** with a high, arched tail. The Saddlebred is a **gaited horse**, which means it can learn to move in ways other breeds of horses cannot.

Colors: The most common colors are **chestnut**, **bay**, brown, and black, but many other colors are also seen.

Development

History of breed: Saddlebreds descend from the ancient English Pacer, with **Thoroughbred** blood added.

Place of origin: Saddlebreds originated in eastern and south-central North America.

Numbers: Over a quarter of a million Saddlebreds are registered, with more than 3,000 added every year.

Life History

Life span: A well-cared-for American Saddlebred may live from 25 to 30 years.

Uses

Saddlebreds are the most popular horses in horse shows. They are also used for hunting, jumping, pleasure riding, endurance riding, and carriage driving.

Chapter 1

The Horse That Explored America

It was late at night on April 18, 1775. A man and horse waited in the dark near Boston Harbor. The man looked toward a church tower across the bay. The man and horse knew each other well. They had traveled many miles together. Tonight, they would make the most important ride of their lives.

A light appeared in the tower. It was the signal they had been waiting for. In an instant, they were off. They galloped across streams

Paul Revere rode a Narragansett Pacer, a forerunner of the American Saddlebred.

American Saddlebreds have many wonderful qualities.

and over bridges. They raced through fields and woods.

Dogs barked and owls hooted. Frightening shadows flew up. The faithful horse galloped mile after mile through the night. At every town and farmhouse the man shouted as loud as he could, "The British are coming!"

The farmers and townspeople were ready when the British soldiers attacked the next morning.

They were ready because of that good horse and his rider. The rider was Paul Revere. His horse was a Narragansett Pacer, the forerunner of the American Saddlebred.

Made in America

Paul Revere trusted a special horse to carry him on his important mission. It was the kind of horse that early settlers bred to travel and explore the rugged American countryside 300 years ago. These horses were intelligent. They had great endurance. They were very comfortable to ride. By the time of the Revolutionary War (1775-1783), they existed only in North America.

Horses that can pace are called gaited horses.

Chapter 2
America Saves the Gaited Horse

All horses have four natural **gaits**. They can walk, **trot, canter**, and **gallop**. The walk gives the smoothest ride, but it is slow. At a trot, a horse can travel faster, but it can be a very bumpy ride. The canter is fast and smooth. The gallop is fastest of all. But horses cannot canter or gallop for very long distances. Both horse and rider tire.

James Fenimore Cooper described pacing horses in his famous book, *The Last of the Mohicans*.

A Smoother Riding Horse

A few breeds of horses are able to move with another gait. It is called the **pace**. Horses that can pace are called pacers or gaited horses. There are different styles of pacing gaits. The style depends on the breeding and training of each horse. Pacers can go as fast as trotters without the bumpy ride of the trot. That is why pacers make good riding horses.

Pacers were popular saddle horses in Europe during the Middle Ages. Rough roads made travel difficult. Almost everyone traveled on horseback. The best gaited horses came from England, Ireland, and Scotland. When colonists came to America, they brought English Pacers with them. There were very few roads in America in the 1600s.

Horses for a Changing World

English Pacers did very well in the American and French colonies of North America. In New England, they were called Narragansett Pacers, after Rhode Island's

American Saddlebreds are easy to recognize.

American Saddlebreds are sturdy, good-natured horses.

Narragansett Bay, where many pacers were raised.
In Canada, they were called Canadian Pacers. Large
farms bred and raised these horses for the new
settlers who arrived every year. James Fenimore
Cooper described these sturdy, good-natured horses
in his famous book, *The Last of the Mohicans.*

In the early 1700s, Narragansetts were carefully
crossbred with Thoroughbreds. The result was a
bigger and faster horse. This improved breed of

gaited horse was first known simply as the American Horse. Colonists explored and settled much of North America on American Horses.

In Europe, gaited horses were no longer popular. By 1775, they had almost disappeared in Europe. There were only a few English Pacers left. These were the Narragansetts, Canadian Pacers, and American Horses in the colonies.

American Saddlebreds display a proud elegance.

Chapter 3

The First American Horse Breed

By the time Paul Revere made his famous ride, the American Horse was the most popular horse in the colonies. Farmers and frontiersmen fought the Revolutionary War on American Horses. They defeated the better-trained British cavalry.

After the Revolutionary War, many pioneers followed frontiersman Daniel Boone. They rode American Horses west into Kentucky and then on to Missouri. There the American Horse grew in beauty and style.

Thoroughbreds and Morgans were mated with American Horses to get the American Saddlebred.

A New Look

The frontier turned into farms and towns. People wanted a horse that was more than just a comfortable ride. Horses had to plow the fields. They had to jump streams and fences for hunting. They had to pull fancy carriages to town on Sundays. People wanted a horse that could do all that, and win a race besides.

Breeders developed a horse that could do all these things. They carefully chose the **sires** and **dams** of the **foals** they raised. They crossbred horses to get the traits they wanted.

Thoroughbred and **Morgan** horses had beauty and speed. They were mated with the American Horses. The outcome was a fine, high-stepping, picture-perfect riding horse.

But these horses were more than beautiful. They kept the strength and smooth gaits of the Narragansetts. They were called American Saddle Horses, Kentucky Saddlers, or Saddlebreds. During the 1800s, they were the most popular riding horses in North America.

American Saddlebreds can be shown in three classes.

Horse shows became major events because more and more people wanted to show off their beautiful Saddlebreds.

War and Danger

During the Civil War (1861-1865), everything changed. Farmers left their fields to fight other Americans. The soldiers brought their own horses with them. They used mostly Saddlebreds. Confederate commanders Robert E. Lee and Stonewall Jackson rode Saddlebreds. Union generals Ulysses S. Grant and William Tecumseh Sherman rode Saddlebreds. The horses became war heroes, too.

Thousands of horses died during the Civil War. Few horses remained on farms in the South. The Saddlebred became an endangered breed.

When the South surrendered in 1865, General Grant issued an order that possibly saved the breed. He allowed each Confederate soldier to take his horse home with him. These

The National Saddle Horse Breeders Association was formed in 1891 in Louisville, Kentucky.

Saddlebreds are known mostly for their beauty and style.

were the strongest and bravest Saddlebreds of all.
They had survived the war. These war horses
became the sires and dams of a new generation of
Saddlebreds.

Saddlebreds Become an Official Breed

After the Civil War, Saddlebred breeders
organized **pedigrees**. Pedigrees are the family trees
of horses. In 1891, breeders from several states met
in Louisville, Kentucky. They formed the National
Saddle Horse Breeders Association. It was the first

official horse breed **registry** in the United States.

Over a quarter of a million Saddlebred horses have been registered. Today the registry is called the American Saddlebred Horse Association. Saddlebreds are now the most popular show horses in North America.

Saddlebreds hold their heads high and proud.

Chapter 4

The Saddlebred Today

After more than 100 years of careful breeding, American Saddlebreds have many wonderful qualities. But today's Saddlebreds are known mostly for their beauty and style.

Classic Beauty

American Saddlebred horses are different from other modern breeds. They have an unusual look that is easy to recognize. When trained and groomed for the show ring, Saddlebreds display a proud elegance. They seem to fulfill everyone's idea of what a classic horse should be.

American Saddlebreds are the most popular show horses in North America.

One of the most noticeable features is the Saddlebred's beautiful head. Saddlebreds hold their heads high and proud. Because their necks are long and flexible, they carry their heads higher than other breeds. Saddlebreds have a straight face line with large, wide-set eyes and flaring nostrils.

In the past, Saddlebred trainers used special gear on their horses. The gear taught the horses to hold their heads even higher than they would naturally. This training had to be done very carefully or the horse's neck would get sore. Today's Saddlebreds are bred to hold their heads high naturally. Trainers do not use the gear very often anymore.

Saddlebreds are quiet and gentle. They are not very high-spirited. When they face something new or unknown, they become extra-alert. They prick up their ears. Their nostrils flare. Their eyes sparkle.

Some owners train their horses to get excited when ridden. They want the horses to act excited in the show ring. But most people

American Saddlebreds carry their heads high.

do not want a horse that gets too excited. They want horses to be safe for trail or pleasure riding.

Tall and Graceful

Saddlebreds are tall. Horses are measured in hands. A hand is four inches (10 centimeters). A horse's height is measured from the withers to the ground. Most Saddlebreds are 15 to 16 hands.

Saddlebreds look slender. But they are very muscular. Saddlebreds weigh between 1,000 and 1,200 pounds (450 to 540 kilograms). Long legs make them look tall and graceful. For the show ring, some people accent this look by allowing their horses' hooves to grow longer than normal. They sometimes put tall horseshoes on their hooves.

Farriers, or horseshoers, must be specially trained in hoof care and shoeing. If a horse is not shod correctly, it could go lame. Putting shoes on a horse when it is too young could damage the horse's feet or legs.

Saddlebreds look slender, but they are very muscular.

Some trainers add small weights to the toe of each front shoe. These weights can weigh up to a pound (half a kilogram). The weights make the horse's feet feel heavier. But the horse must pick them up just as high to walk or run normally.

When the horse arrives at a horse show, the weights are taken off. Because the horse is used to having heavy hooves, it will pick up its feet extra-high because its feet feel so light. Some trainers use rubber cords or even chains between the horse's two front ankles for the same purpose. This method is not as common as weights.

When horses are wearing these special shoes, they cannot run in a pasture because they could hurt themselves or another horse. They must stay in their stalls. They can only be ridden on level ground such as in a riding ring. Saddlebreds used for trail and pleasure riding wear ordinary horseshoes or none at all.

Saddlebred riders wear dressy outfits.

Tail Nicking

One of the most beautiful features of a Saddlebred horse is its long, flowing tail. It arches up naturally when the horse moves. Some people add special hairpieces to make the horses' **manes** or tails look even longer. Some Saddlebred owners have **veterinarians** do surgery to make their horses' tails arch up higher. This surgery is called nicking.

Tail nicking was a common practice in the 1800s. Horse and buggy travel was the main form of transportation. Most horses that pulled carriages had to wear **cruppers**. A crupper is a loop of leather or nylon that fits around the base of the horse's tail. The crupper is an important part of the driving horse's **harness**. The crupper keeps the entire harness in place so it will not become twisted. A twisted harness could make the horse stumble and tip the carriage.

If a horse's tail sits too low, the crupper can be uncomfortable or even cause sores. A horse with a high-arching tail has more room for the

American Saddlebreds are beautiful and intelligent.

crupper and is less likely to get sore. In the
past, nicking was a way to stretch the tail
higher for horses that had to wear cruppers.
Today nicking is done only for show.

A veterinarian nicks a horse's tail when the
horse is about a year old. The veterinarian cuts

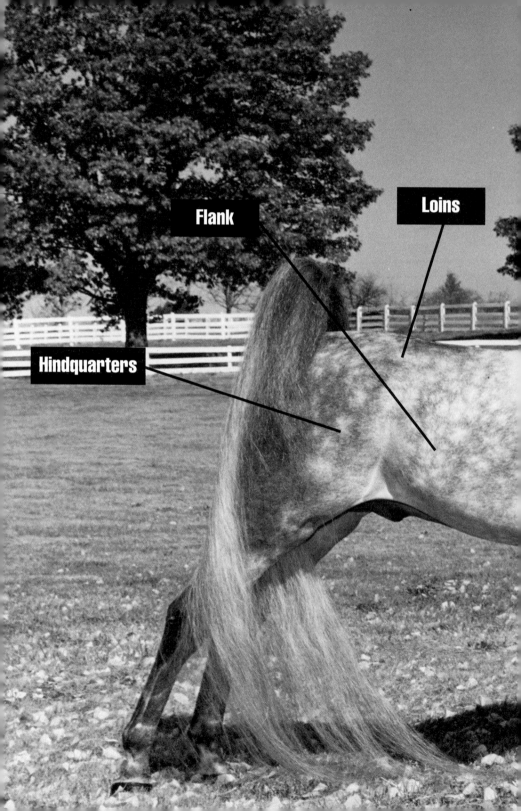

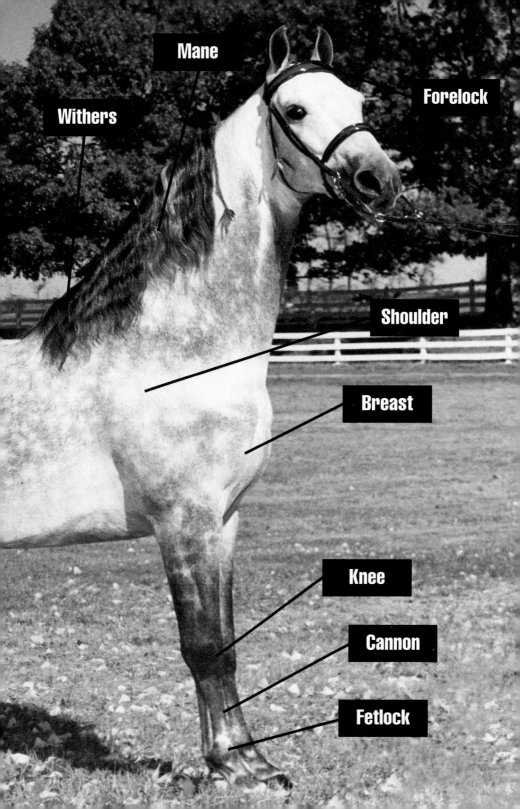

two small ligaments, one on each side, just below the base of the tail. With these ligaments cut, the tail is able to stretch up higher. A special brace is fastened around the base of the tail to keep the tail up. The young horse must wear the brace most of the time for several years, or the ligaments might grow back together. After a few years the brace can come off. The horse will usually continue to hold its tail high.

Nicking is still common at horse shows. But fewer and fewer Saddlebred owners are nicking their horses. Many veterinary schools no longer teach students how to nick tails.

Saddlebreds are easy winners at horse shows.

Chapter 5
Saddlebreds in Action

Saddlebred horses are the most popular horses in horse shows. They have beauty, intelligence, spirit, and special gaits. All this makes them winners in many different types of competition.

Dressage is where the Saddlebred truly shines. Dressage is a complicated style of riding in which horse and rider move together. They communicate with each other through voice and touch. Saddlebreds are very good at dressage.

Style and appearance are also important in dressage. Saddlebreds are easy winners. Riders

Saddlebreds are becoming popular outside of shows.

wear dressy outfits. They put their best **tack** on the horses. Some horses wear fancy ribbons or braids in their manes.

Horses are ridden around an oval ring. They perform turns and other tricks at various gaits. Show officials shout commands at the horses and riders. They tell them when to turn, change gaits, or stop. Judges rate each horse's performance.

Dressage Classes for Saddlebreds

Saddlebreds are shown in three-gaited, five-gaited, and harness classes. In the three-gaited class, horses travel around the ring at a walk, trot, and canter. Each of these gaits can be done in various styles. The rider tells the horse which foot to begin with for each style. The horse must travel a straight path, go the right speed, and step high.

In the five-gaited class, the horse performs two of the special pacing gaits that only gaited breeds are able to do. These are the **slow gait** and the **rack**. The slow gait is a dancing walk-trot. The rack is a full-speed, fancy prance.

In the harness class, Saddlebreds pull small, open buggies around the ring at the walk and trot.

Saddlebreds are among the most comfortable horses to ride, whether it is for show or fun.

They must also show that they can stand quietly while hitched to the buggy. The best Saddlebreds can pull a buggy just as well as they can carry a rider.

Saddlebreds still have the heart and soul of the horses
that explored America 300 years ago.

Saddlebreds on the Trail

Though they are best known as a show
breed, Saddlebred horses are still used for farm
and ranch work, just as they were a century
ago. Saddlebreds still carry riders safely over
forest trails. They still pull elegant carriages
down country roads.

Because of their pacing ancestry, Saddlebreds are among the most comfortable horses to ride. Their popularity is growing among people who enjoy trail riding through the countryside. Some trail riders say that once they rode their first Saddlebred, they never wanted to ride any other horse. Their cool ability to handle challenges makes Saddlebreds good trail horses.

Another event that is gaining popularity is **endurance riding**. It is also called long-distance trail riding. Endurance riding is a planned race that covers from 25 to 100 miles (40 to 160 kilometers) and lasts for several days. Endurance riding began in North America. It is now popular in Europe, Australia, and South Africa.

Saddlebreds have the strength and dependability to win endurance events. American Saddlebred Horses still have the heart and soul of the horses that explored America 300 years ago.

Glossary

bay—a reddish-brown horse with black legs, mane, and tail

canter—a slow running gait

chestnut—a reddish-brown horse

croup—the rump, or back portion of the upper back, of a horse

crupper—a loop that passes around a horse's tail and attaches to a harness or saddle

dam—the mother of a horse

dressage (dreh-SAZH)—a competition in which horses receive complicated commands from their riders

farrier—a person who trims and cares for horses' hooves, makes horseshoes, and shoes horses

foal—a young horse

gait— a way a horse can move its feet to travel

gaited horse—a horse that can travel in special ways that other horses cannot

gallop—the fastest movement of a horse

hand—a unit of measurement equal to four inches (10 centimeters)

harness—the set of straps, usually made of leather or nylon, that a horse wears to pull something

mane—the long hair growing on the top of a horse's head and down the neck

Morgan—a breed of horse descended from one famous stallion from Vermont

nicking—the practice of cutting ligaments in a horse's tail to make it arch higher

pace—any of several special gaits natural to only certain breeds of horses

pedigree—a list of a horse's ancestors

rack—a fast, specialized gait in which each foot strikes the ground separately, one after the other

registry—an organization that keeps track of official pedigrees for a particular horse breed

sire—the father of a horse

slow gait—a prancing-type gait in which one foot after the other is lifted and then held momentarily in midair

tack—the various equipment worn by horses for handling, training, riding, and driving

Thoroughbred—a breed of racing horse that was bred in England

trot—a medium-fast step natural to all horses, easily recognized by its up-and-down action

veterinarian—a person trained and qualified to treat diseases and injuries of animals

withers—the top of a horse's shoulders

To Learn More

Bidd, Jackie. *Horses.* New York: Kingfisher, 1995.

Edwards, Elwyn Hartley. *Encyclopedia of the Horse.* New York: Dorling Kindersley, 1994.

Henry, Marguerite. *Album of Horses.* New York: Rand McNally, 1951.

Kidd, Jane. *Encyclopedia of Horses and Ponies.* New York: Macmillan, 1995.

Patent, Dorothy Hinshaw. *Horses of America.* New York: Holiday House, 1981.

Price, Steven. *Whole Horse Catalog.* New York: Brigadore Press, 1977.

Taylor, Louis. *The Horse America Made: The Story of the American Saddle Horse.* New York: Harper & Row, 1961.

You can read articles about American Saddlebred Horses in the following magazines: *American Saddlebred, Just About Horses, Saddle Horse Report, Young Equestrian,* and *Young Rider.*

Useful Addresses

American Horse Council
1700 K Street NW, Suite 300
Washington, DC 20006-3805

American Horse Publications
2946 Carriage Drive
South Daytona, FL 32119

**American Saddlebred Horse Association
and American Saddle Horse Museum**
4093 Iron Works Pike
Lexington, KY 40511-8434

American Saddlebred Horse Association of Canada
2150 Rashdale Road
Armstrong, BC V0E 1B0
Canada

American Youth Horse Council
4193 Iron Works Pike
Lexington, KY 40511-2742

Index